W9-BVM-140

Anna Tomacek

Viennese
Specialties

KOMPASS **Kitchen Delights**

Before you begin!

Vienna's cuisine is the only cuisine known throughout the entire world that takes its name from a large international city. Its special character stems from the fact that Vienna was once the capital of a huge empire encompassing many peoples and cultures. The imperial court and its aristocracy left a lasting impression on the city with its expressions, table etiquette and culinary habits. Vienna's geographic location and court politics brought various influences to play over the centuries. Italian, Turkish, Hungarian, Bohemian, and even Romanian national dishes were taken over by Viennese cuisine and adapted to meet local tastes. Thus, Goulash and Paprika Chicken originated in Hungary, while the world-famous Wiener Schnitzel comes from Milan, Italy. Field Marshal Radetzky supposedly brought the recipe for „costoletta milanese" to Vienna in 1848. The dumplings, particularly the Palffy Dumplings (rolled bread dumplings) come from Bohemia. „Palatschinken" (crepes, pancakes) have been a staple of Viennese cuisine since the 19th century. Their origins are especially interesting: originally made in Romania and known as „placinta" (or flat cakes), the Hungarians adopted them as „palacinta." The Viennese then took them over, and the name of this delicious pastry

became „palatschinken."
In addition to these ethnic influences, Viennese cuisine also has a number of its own typical dishes that are top-ranking favorites in Vienna. Included among these ever-popular dishes are „Tafelspitz" (boiled beef brisket), Viennese Steak and Onions, and the famous Sacher Torte. In this book you will find a wide range of traditional recipes, including soups, diverse fish, meat and poultry dishes, side dishes as well as pastries,

breads, and finally coffee specialties. I have also included the origins of some of these dishes. The following pages describe some outstanding Viennese specialties. These are followed by some cooking and kitchen terms. This is sure to make it easy to get to know the multi-faceted Viennese cuisine and to try your hand at some of its delicacies. As always, I wish you the best success.

Yours,

Anna Tomacek

Contents
Page

Before You Begin! 2

Viennese Specialties - A Brief Overview. 4

Essential Kitchen Terms 7

Soups 10

Fish 18

Meats and Poultry 23

Dumplings, Side Dishes and Salads 48

Desserts 57

Doughnuts 76/94

Pastries 83

Viennese Coffee Primer 95

Viennese Specialties -
A Brief Overview

Over the centuries, Austria's capital city of Vienna became the hub of a rich and multifaceted cuisine. A patchwork of the most diverse nationalities and ethnic influences, Vienna amazingly melded the „cooking pot and the culture." This is illustrated by the diversity of Viennese cuisine. Ever-popular are clear **soups** containing diverse noodles or pastries.

Here, the preparation of a hearty **beef stock** is at the core. This soup is not only used as a stock for soups, but also to baste other dishes. Having time and patience are the first prerequisites for successful cooking. Just as important are good ingredients, particularly the meats you select, for example beef with a soup bone. Hearty appetizer soups are created by adding dumplings, pasta, pastries, such as the „Schöberln", tiny pastries of flour and egg, or **Semolina Dumplings**.The selection of **fish** is also diverse, particularly fresh-water fish, available at Vienna markets. A particular favorite is „Fogosch" (Hungarian for perch-pike). If such a fish is caught in the Danube, it is called „Schill." Other popular fish include **pike** and **carp**. The Viennese also love their **meat dishes**, and the Viennese certainly eat more meat than do other parts of Austria. For this reason, the meat dishes are given a particularly long chapter. The extensive Viennese „beef culture" is the foundation of many recipes.

Portions are always generous. Without question, one of the best beef dishes is the „**Tafelspitz**" - a special loin cut, which is often served with apple horseradish. History has it that Tafelspitz was a particular favorite of Emperor Franz Joseph I. „**Lungenbraten**" (Braised Beef Tenderloin) and other **roast beef** variations (Steak and Onion Roast, Vanilla Steak or Esterhazy Steak) are also popular beef dishes. Viennese cuisine also boasts the „**Stelze**," or Grilled Pork Hock, as well as **Goulash**, and the thinly pounded „**Vienna Schnitzel**." Other typical dishes are „Beuschel" (veal lung stew), and poultry specialties such as „**Viennese Fried Chicken**" and „**Paprika Chicken**." Meat dishes are accompanied by diverse **side dishes**, such as „Vogerlsalat" (Lamb's Lettuce Salad), green beans, cauliflower or hearty dumplings. Served hot or cold, **pastries and desserts** play a major role in Viennese cuisine. For the most part, these hearty dishes originated at the peasant table and found their way to the capital city, where they evolved into delightful fantasies of egg white and meringue, sugar and other ingredients, and no longer serve as main dishes but rather desserts.

A particular specialty of Viennese cuisine are the „Koche" - a type of sweet, oven-baked or fried casserole. **Wine Pudding, Viennese Bread Pudding** and **Kipferl Casserole** are three well-known examples. **Palatschinken**, or Viennese crepes, are filled with a wide variety of things and are just as popular as desserts as the famous **Viennese Apple Strudel, Emperor's Pancake,** and **Yeast Dumplings.**

The Viennese also love their **doughnuts,** such as the „Schlosserbuam" and „Wäschermadln," all traditionally made and eaten during Carnival and Lent. The final chapter of the book is devoted to **Viennese pastries.** Who has not heard of or tasted the melt-in-your-mouth **Viennese Vanilla Crescents,** the tender **Emperor's Gugelhupf,** or the world-renowned **Sacher Torte?**

The Viennese eat and drink with gusto. Nevertheless, **coffee** is much more than a mere beverage - it is part of the city's tradition. The preferred locale in which to enjoy a cup is one of the countless Viennese coffeehouses. Depending on your taste, you can order a „Melange" (coffee with milk), usually crowned with a cap of whipped cream, an „Einspanner" (double mocha with whipped cream), or **Turkish coffee,** prepared and served in a tiny coffee pot. No matter where you decide to dine or drink, there is no more wonderful atmosphere than in Vienna, the city of „gemütlichkeit."

Essential Kitchen Terms

Douse   To quickly add hot liquid to frying meat or vegetables, for instance to loosen pan drippings

Rinse   To rinse boiled foods, such as spaetzle, with cold water to prevent sticking and halt the cooking process

Drain   To place food in a colander or sieve and let drip off

Roll Out   To roll out dough

Roux   Butter and flour mixture, heated slowly

Grind   To pass meat through a grinder

Let Rise   To place a yeast dough in a bowl, cover with a dry dishtowel, and let stand in a warm place, until it has almost doubled in size

Bind   To bind a fluid with egg yolk, cream or butter

Mill   To press through a fine sieve or use a blender to finely purée potatoes

Grate   To grate coarsely

Let Rest   To let dough stand and „rest"

Reduce   To boil until thickened; sauces or pan drippings are thickened by evaporation to bring out their flavors more intensely

Beat   To beat ingredients into a foamy consistency using an egg-beater

Fold   To carefully mix beaten egg whites and batter. The best way to do this is using a spatula, lifting the batter over the egg whites and gently mixing until well combined.

Beat   To briefly beat egg

Simmer   To allow delicate dishes to continue cooking below the boiling point

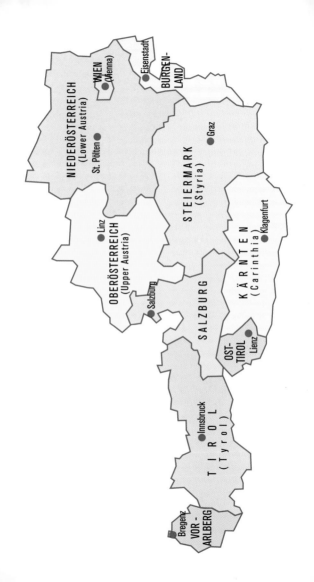

NIEDERÖSTERREICH
(Lower Austria)
St. Pölten

WIEN
(Vienna)

Eisenstadt

BURGEN-
LAND

STEIERMARK
(Styria)

Graz

OBERÖSTERREICH
(Upper Austria)

Linz

KÄRNTEN
(Carinthia)

Klagenfurt

Salzburg

SALZBURG

OST-
TIROL

Lienz

Innsbruck

T I R O L
(T y r o l)

Bregenz

VOR-
ARLBERG

KOMPASS

1716 Viennese Specialties
1717 Austrian Pastries and Desserts
1719 Tyrolean Specialties
1743 Dumplings
1762 Tuscan Specialties

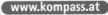

www.kompass.at

Emperor's Dumpling Soup
(Kaiserschöberlsuppe)

3 egg whites	butter and flour for cookie sheet
pinch of salt	6 cups hot beef stock
3 egg yolks	salt, pepper
½ cup flour	chopped parsley

● Preheat oven to 350° F.

● Beat egg whites until stiff. Quickly mix in beaten egg yolks, salt and sifted flour.

● Grease and dust a small cake form or cookie sheet. Spread batter ½ inch thick and bake for 12-17 min or until golden brown. Let cool, then cut into 1-inch squares.

● In the meantime, heat and ladle beef soup into bowls. Add several squares and sprinkle with freshly chopped parsley. Serve immediately.

Beef Soup with Semolina Dumplings
(Rindssuppe mit Griessnockerln)

For the beef soup:	For the semolina dumplings:
6 - 8 cups water, salt	2 oz butter
1 oz beef liver	1 egg
1 carrot	approx. ⅓ cup semolina
1 parsley root	salt, white pepper
¼ celery root	freshly grated nutmeg to taste
1 onion	
approx. 1 ¾ lb soup meat	approx. 8 cups salted water
approx. ½ lb beef and marrow bones, chopped	1 T freshly chopped parsley

For the beef soup:

● Clean, peel and chop soup vegetables. Place in a large pot and cover with cold water. Bring to a boil and then add salt. Add chopped beef bones and marrow bones and finely chopped liver.

● Bring to a boil, then add soup meat, which has first been rinsed under cold water. Skim off foam and reduce heat. Simmer about 2 hours.

● Remove meat and bones. Drain soup through a sieve. Use meat separately.

For the Semolina Dumplings:

● Beat butter in a bowl until creamy. Add egg, salt and semolina, as well as pepper, and if desired, freshly grated nutmeg. Let mixture stand about 30 min.

● Dip a teaspoon in water, scoop dumplings and gently drop into boiling salted water. Reduce heat. Cover and let dumplings steam for 15 - 20 min.

● Remove dumplings from salted water with a slotted spoon, distribute to bowls and cover with hot beef soup. Garnish with freshly chopped parsley and serve immediately.

Beef Soup with Pancake Strips
(Fritattensuppe)

Pancake batter:	Soup:
½ cup flour	6 cups beef broth
pinch of salt, 1 - 2 eggs	salt
½ cup milk	pepper
some mineral water	freshly chopped parsley
3 - 4 T butter or margarine to fry pancakes	or chives

● Sift flour and salt into a bowl. Beat in eggs. Mix milk with mineral water and slowly stir to a smooth batter. Beat with a hand mixer until smooth. Let batter stand for 30 min.

● Heat butter or margarine in a small skillet or omelet pan. Using a ladle, pour batter into skillet and rotate until batter covers base of pan. When one side is golden brown, turn and brown other side. Continue with remaining batter.

● Roll pancakes and slice into thin strips. Distribute into preheated soup plates or bowls and cover with hot beef soup. Garnish with freshly chopped parsley or chives.

Lung Strudel Soup
(Lungenstrudelsuppe)

Strudel dough:	some chopped parsley
½ cup flour	1 oz butter
some oil, vinegar	1 egg
pinch of salt	salt, pepper, marjoram
1 egg yolk	6 cups salted water for boiling
approx. ¼ cup water	
1 egg	
	Soup:
Filling:	6 cups strong, hot beef soup
9 oz boiled veal or pig lung	salt, pepper
1 medium onion	chopped parsley

● Sift flour into a bowl. Create a well in the middle. Add oil, vinegar, salt and egg yolk. Use a mixer to knead to a smooth dough, adding as much water as needed to make a medium-firm dough. Continue kneading by hand until the dough has a silky sheen.

Cover and let stand for 30 min.

● In the meantime, prepare filling. Cut lung into narrow strips and place in a bowl. Add finely chopped, sautéed onions and chopped parsley. Stir in egg, pepper, salt and marjoram.

● Place strudel dough on a large, flour-dusted cloth and roll out very thinly. Using the back of your hands, pull the dough outward from the center. Cut off thicker dough edges.

● Spread filling onto two-thirds of the dough surface. Using the cloth and starting on the side with the filling, form the strudel by rolling the dough to the side without the filling, which has been covered with beaten egg.

● Using a floured wooden spoon, divide the strudel into small squares, cut through with the back of a knife, and press edges firmly together. Place gently in boiling salted water and let simmer for 12 - 15 min.

● Remove strudel pieces from water and place in soup bowls or plates. Immediately cover with hot beef soup. Garnish with freshly chopped parsley and serve.

Beef Soup with Spleen Slices
(Rindssuppe mit Milzschnitten)

For the Spleen Slices:

1 small onion

some chopped parsley

¼ cup oil for frying

1½ oz butter

1 egg

3 oz beef spleen

salt

pepper

nutmeg

2 Kaiser rolls or 4 slices white bread

4 oz shortening for deep frying

For the soup:

6 cups beef broth

Freshly chopped parsley to taste

● Sauté chopped onion and parsley in oil. Let cool. Beat together butter and egg until creamy. Add finely chopped and puréed spleen, salt, pepper and nutmeg. Spread this mixture about ¼ inch thick on thinly sliced Kaiser roll or white bread.

14

● Place in hot shortening or oil, topping side down, and fry until golden brown. Remove and let drain. Place in hot beef soup while still warm. If desired, garnish with freshly chopped parsley. Serve immediately.

Tomato Soup
(Tomatensuppe)

1 medium onion	2 cups beef stock
1 small parsley root	salt, white pepper
1½ oz butter	pinch of sugar
1 lb ripe tomatoes	some dry red wine
1 oz butter	1 T lemon juice
⅓ cup flour	2 - 3 T sour cream
3 cups cold water	cooked rice if desired

● Peel and finely chop onion and parsley root. Sauté in butter. Scald tomatoes, dip in cold water and peel. Chop finely and add to onion/parsley mixture. Simmer and then pass through a coarse sieve.

● Melt butter in a larger pot. Stir in flour and let brown slightly. Slowly add water and using a wire whisk, beat until smooth. Add beef stock and bring to a boil, stirring constantly. Simmer over low heat for 15 - 20 min, then add tomato mixture.

● Season to taste with salt, pepper, sugar, red wine and lemon juice.

● Heat again, remove from burner and stir in sour cream. If desired, add precooked rice to make tomato rice soup.

Viennese Potato Soup
(Wiener Erdäpfelsuppe)

2 carrots	4 cups beef stock
¼ celery root	white pepper
1 small parsley root	1 - 2 T flour
1 onion	cold water
2 - 3 T butter	6 - 8 T sour cream
1 lb potatoes	1 clove garlic
salt, some marjoram	2 boiled potatoes
ground caraway seed	1 T freshly chopped chives
approx. 2 cups water	to taste

● Peel and finely dice carrot, celery root, parsley root, onion and potatoes. Sauté root vegetables in hot butter, then add potatoes.

Add salt, season with caraway and marjoram. Cover with water. Simmer until tender, about 35 - 45 min, stirring occasionally.

● Then strain the mixture through a sieve, return to pot, add beef stock and heat. Season with pepper and thicken with flour, which was stirred into cold water.

● Season to taste. Stir in sour cream. Peel and, using a garlic press, add garlic. Add diced boiled potatoes. If desired, garnish with freshly chopped chives.

Liver Dumpling Soup
(Leberknödelsuppe)

1 small onion	pepper
1 oz butter	marjoram
½ bunch parsley, chopped	pinch of nutmeg
¼ lb ground beef liver	½ clove garlic
2 stale rolls	bread crumbs as needed
1 egg	4 cups beef stock
salt	chives

● Peel and finely chop onions. Heat butter in a skillet. Add onions and parsley. Sauté, stirring constantly. Remove from heat.

● Place liver in a mixing bowl. Soak stale rolls in water, squeeze out excess liquid and tear apart, adding small pieces to bowl. Combine with egg, seasoning, pressed garlic, and onion/parsley mixture.

● Stir until mixture is smooth, using a hand mixer with dough hooks. If the mixture is too soft or liquid, add some bread crumbs.

● Let stand about 30 min. With wet hands, form oval dumplings and, depending on their size, simmer for 10 - 15 min in boiling salted water. Remove and drain well. Place in hot beef soup, garnish with chopped chives and serve immediately.

Deep-Fried Carp
(Gebackener Karpfen)

4 slices of fresh carp, each approx. ¼ - ½ lb	approx. 8 T bread crumbs (for breading fish)
salt	generous amount of short-ening for frying
4 -5 T flour	parsley
2 - 3 eggs	lemon slices

● Rinse fish under cold, running water and pat dry with paper towels. Score skin to ensure that fish fries thoroughly.

● Salt on both sides. Dip in flour, then beaten egg, and finally, cover with bread crumbs.

● Heat shortening in a large skillet. Reduce heat.

Fry fish on both sides until golden brown.

● Remove fish, drain well. Serve immediately, garnishing fish with fresh parsley sprigs and lemon slices.

Our tip:
Serve carp with Viennese Potato Salad. You'll find the recipe on page 53.

Fish Aspic
(Fischsulz)

200 g carrots	1 bay leaf
1 cup beef stock	scant 2 lbs fish fillets
1½ cups dry white wine	1 egg white
salt, 6 black pepper corns, crushed	some lemon juice
3 allspice berries	8 - 9 leaves of clear gelatin
2 whole cloves, 2 juniper berries	1 hard-boiled egg
	5 black olives
	freshly chopped dill

- Clean carrots and place whole in hot beef stock. Simmer until tender, about 20 min. Remove, drain and let cool. Add white wine and seasonings to soup and simmer for about 10 min.

- Rinse fish fillets under cold, running water. Pat dry with paper towels and place in hot broth. Simmer for about 15 min and carefully remove. Let cool.

- Strain broth through a sieve. Fold in stiffly beaten egg white and bring to a boil. Skim off foam and pour broth through a sieve lined with cheesecloth or filter paper to clarify the broth.

- Season to taste with lemon juice. Add softened leaves of gelatin to hot broth, stirring until dissolved.

- Slice carrot and egg.

- Rinse rectangular form with cold water. Pour in about ½ inch of broth. Move form to spread gelatin mixture to thinly cover sides and bottom. Place form in refrigerator to harden.

- When gelatin has hardened, decorate sides and bottom with sliced olives, egg and carrot. Add more gelatin mixture and let harden. Place fish pieces, dill and remaining garnishes on top of second layer and fill form with remaining gelatin mixture. Cool for 4 - 5 hours.

- When serving, dip form briefly in hot water and turn form over onto a plate.

Our tip:
Fish Aspic tastes best with pan-fried potatoes.

20

Delicate Pike Dumplings

(Feine Hechtnockerl)

approx. 5 oz white bread without crusts	pinch of freshly grated nutmeg
1 cup whipping cream	salt
1 small onion	white pepper
2 T butter	4 cups fish stock (or salted water)
1 lb pike fillets	green salad and caviar to garnish
1 egg white	

● Dice white bread. Cover with whipping cream. Stir and let stand.

● Peel and very finely chop onion. Sauté until clear in butter. Let cool.

● Check fillets for bones. Rinse briefly under cold running water and pat dry with paper towels. Purée in food processor.

● Mix puréed fish with sautéed onion, white bread, whipping cream and egg white until a smooth mixture is formed. Season well with nutmeg, salt and pepper and place in refrigerator to chill.

Heat fish stock or salted water. Form dumplings with teaspoons dipped in hot water. Place these gently in hot, but not boiling, stock or salted water.

● Immediately reduce heat and cook dumplings for 15 - 20 min, until done.

● In the meantime, clean and drain lettuce and mixed greens. Add vinegar, oil and seasonings to taste. Place on plates. Remove dumplings and place on plates. Garnish with caviar and serve.

Serve with:
Toasted white bread.

Stuffed Pike-Perch
(Gefüllter Fogosch)

2 lbs cleaned perch	1½ oz diced bacon
juice of ½ lemon	chopped parsley
salt,	white pepper
pepper	pinch of cayenne pepper

Filling:	For baking / roasting:
1 stale roll or 2 slices white bread	¼ lb bacon strips
1 - 2 T hot milk	¼ cup melted butter
1 onion	1 cup cream
1 oz butter	½ cup dry white wine
	½ lb fresh mushrooms

● Clean the fish. Rinse under cold, running water and pat dry with paper towel. Mix lemon juice, salt and pepper, and rub the inside and outside of the fish with the mixture. Let stand approx. 15 min.

● For the stuffing:
Finely slice rolls. Put in a bowl, drizzle with hot milk. Sauté onion, bacon and parsley and add to roll mixture. Stuff fish and close opening with toothpicks.

● Preheat oven to 350° F.

● Before baking, „lard" both sides of the fish with bacon strips. Place in suitable baking pan and bake. After about 10 min, baste with melted butter and let bake another 20 - 30 min.

● While fish is baking, pour cream and white wine over fish. Baste occasionally with juice in pan.

● Clean and finely slice mushrooms. Add to fish 5 - 10 min before end of baking time and bake along with fish.

● Remove baking pan from oven. Carefully remove fish and place on serving platter. Season sauce to taste and serve with fish.

Steamed Tenderloin in Cream Sauce
(Gedämpfter Lungenbraten in Rahmsoße)

1½ lb beef tenderloin	½ - 1 cup beef broth
salt, pepper	½ bay leaf
2 oz butter	thyme
1 onion, finely chopped	several crushed black peppercorns
⅛ celery root, diced	some lemon juice
1 small carrot, finely sliced	½ cup mushrooms sautéed in butter
⅛ cup flour	
½ cup sour cream	

● If necessary, remove skin from tenderloin. Rinse under cold, running water and pat dry with paper towel. Season on all sides and brown in butter. Remove and place on platter.

● Sauté onion, celery root and carrots in same skillet. Sprinkle with flour. Cover with cream and stock. Add seasonings, lemon juice and tenderloin.

● Cover and simmer for about 1 hour. Turn meat occasionally.

● Remove meat, slice and place on platter. Keep warm.

● Strain sauce, add mushrooms and bring to a boil.

Serve with:
Rice, green salad

Breaded Veal Cutlets
(Wiener Schnitzel)

4 veal cutlets, approx. 6 - 7 oz each	approx. 1 cup (8 oz) oil
2 eggs, beaten	4 T flour
2 T cream	4 oz bread crumbs
salt	softened butter
white pepper	lemon slices and fresh parsley (garnish)

● Rinse the veal cutlets under cold water, pat dry with paper towel. Cut off any membrane or fat around edges to prevent curling. Pound cutlets on both sides with a cleaver. In a shallow bowl or pie pan, mix well eggs, cream, salt and pepper. Spread bread crumbs in a pie pan.

● Heat oil in a large skillet. Put flour on a plate, add salt and pepper, and dredge both sides of cutlets. Dip cutlets in egg mixture, then coat with bread crumbs.

● One after the other, place breaded cutlets in the hot oil over medium heat and fry for 3 - 5 min turning occasionally. While cooking, carefully rotate the pan to ensure that the oil reaches all parts of the cutlets.

● When both sides are golden brown, remove from oil and drain on absorbent paper. You can also brush melted butter on the „Schnitzel" before serving.

● Typically, Wiener Schnitzel is served with lemon wedges or slices and garnished with parsley.

Serve with:
Potato salad

F.Y.I.
Wiener Schnitzel is a
classic of Viennese cuisine.
It has become popular
as such all over the world,
even though it originates
from Milan, Italy.
Field Marshal Radetzky
is said to have brought
the recipe for „costoletta
milanese" back to
Vienna in 1848.

Steak and Onions
(Wiener Zwiebelrostbraten)

2 medium onions
2 T flour
4 sirloin steaks, approx. 7 oz. each
salt
white pepper
5 T oil
½ cup (4 oz) beef stock
1 T butter
4 small pickles (garnish)

● Peel onions and cut into thin rings. Heat butter in a small frying pan and sauté the onion rings at medium heat until they are a crisp golden brown. Remove from heat and set aside. Remove onion rings and place on a plate. Keep warm.

● Rinse steaks under cold water, dry with paper towel and pound flat with a cleaver. Rub both sides of meat with salt and pepper. While doing this, heat oil in a large, heavy skillet.

● Put flour on a flat plate. Dip one side of meat in flour, shake to remove excess and place in oil, floured side down. Sauté meat, allowing 4 - 6 min per side.

Meat should still be somewhat pink inside (medium).

● Remove steaks to a warmed serving platter. Add broth to skillet in which steaks were cooked and bring to a boil (you can also add butter remaining from the onions, if you wish). Season to taste. Pour over steaks.

● Add onion rings to steaks. Sliced pickles can also be used for garnish.

Serve with:
pan-fried potatoes, steamed vegetables

Esterhazy Steak
(Esterhazy Rostbraten)

4 sirloin steaks, approx. 7 oz each or 2 lbs beef tenderloin	1 medium onion
	pinch of flour
black pepper, salt	pinch of sweet paprika powder
2 - 3 T flour	
4 - 5 T oil	¼ cup (2 oz) meat stock or water
9 oz fresh vegetables (e.g. 1 - 2 carrots, 1 small leek, 2 celery sticks)	juice of ½ lemon
	½ cup (4 oz) sour cream

● Rinse steaks in cold water, pat dry with paper towel. Slash edges to prevent curling.

● Rub both sides of steak with salt and freshly ground black pepper. Dredge one side in flour, shake off excess.

● Heat oil in a large skillet. Sauté steaks, floured side first, at medium heat for 4 - 6 min per side. Meat should still be pink inside (medium).

● Meanwhile, clean and finely slice carrots, leek, celery root and onions.

● Remove meat from skillet, place on warm platter and cover.

● Sauté vegetables in the same skillet. Season with paprika and dust with flour.

● Add some broth or water and simmer until vegetables are tender. Add lemon juice and sour cream; remove skillet from heat.

● Return steaks to the skillet, let stand for several min and serve.

Serve with:
Wide, flat nodles

Vanilla Steak
(Vanille-Rostbraten)

4 sirloin steaks, approx. 8 oz (½ lb) each	1 medium onion
salt	1 - 2 carrots
black pepper	½ cup beef stock
2 T flour	1 - 2 T butter
2 oz butter or lard	1 - 2 cloves of garlic

● Rinse steaks under cold running water and pat dry with paper towel. Slash edges to prevent curling.

● Season on both sides. Dredge one side in flour.

● Heat oil or butter in large skillet. Brown steaks, floured side first, 8 - 10 min per side. Remove from skillet and keep warm. Sauté peeled and finely chopped onion and julienned carrot in same skillet.

● Add broth and butter. Let simmer.

● Peel and finely chop garlic cloves. Sprinkle over steaks, cover with sauce and serve immediately.

Serve with:
Roasted potatoes, steamed onions and spinach.

F.Y.I.
In Viennese cuisine, the term „Rostbraten" always connotes an approximately ½-inch thick slice of beef, usually weighing about ½ lb and cut from the rib like roast beef. The slices are always sautéed in oil, brown outside, pink inside. There are many varieties of this standard dish. This book presents the most wel known: Viennese Steak & Onions, Esterhazy Steak and Vanilla Steak. For some reason, the „vanilla" in this recipe is traditionally garlic.

Veal Lights
("Salonbeuschel," Kalbsbeuschel)

1½ - 2 lb veal lights (lungs)	2 - 3 gherkins
1 medium onion	1 small onion, chopped
5 crushed peppercorns	freshly chopped parsley
1 carrot	grated peel of one untreated lemon
1 parsley root	1 clove garlic
½ celery root	1 sardine fillet
1 small leek	1 tsp capers, finely chopped
4 - 6 cups water	2 oz butter
1 whole clove	some dry white wine
1 bay leaf	1 T each vinegar and lemon juice
1 sprig thyme	

1 cup whipping cream

2 - 3 T sour cream

salt

white pepper

● Thoroughly wash veal lungs and remove any residual blood. Peel onion and cut in half. Clean and peel parsley root, celery root and leek. Chop coarsely. Place all these ingredients in a large pot and cover with water. Add peppercorns, cloves, bay leaf and thyme. Bring to a boil, reduce heat and simmer for 1½ - 2 hours. Drain through colander, saving about ½ liter of stock.

● Remove lung and let cool, weighted down with a cutting board. Cut into short, narrow strips. Chop gherkins. Sauté chopped onion with parsley, lemon peel, pressed garlic, sardine fillet and capers in butter. Douse with white wine, vinegar and lemon juice. Fill pan with stock and simmer for 10 - 15 min. Add lung strips and chopped gherkins. Mix well and heat uncovered for 10 min. Stir whipping cream into sour cream and add just before serving.

● Season well with salt and pepper.

Serve with:
Viennese Bread Dumplings

Boiled Beef with Apple-Horseradish Sauce

(Tafelspitz mit Apfelkren)

---

approx. 2 lbs of beef bones

---

4 ½ lbs loin of beef or beef brisket

---

1 small parsley root, coarsely chopped

---

1 - 2 carrots, coarsely chopped

---

2 celery sticks, coarsely chopped

---

1 small leek

---

2 garlic cloves, crushed

---

2 small onions

---

1 bay leaf

---

3 T chives, finely chopped

---

pinch of nutmeg

---

salt

Sauce:

2 medium apples

---

2 T wine vinegar

---

2 - 3 T grated horseradish

---

1 - 2 tsp sugar

---

pinch of salt, white pepper

● Rinse beef soup bones and place in a large pot. Cover with water, add salt and bring to a boil. Add beef. Bring to a boil and skim the liquid, several times if necessary. Reduce heat.

● Meanwhile, clean, peel (if necessary) and coarsely chop parsley root, carrots, celery root and leek. Peel and quarter onions and garlic cloves. Add vegetables, bay leaf and salt to soup. Again, bring

to a boil and skim.

● Simmer in covered pot for about 2 hours, or until beef can be easily pierced with a sharp knife point. During the last half hour before serving, prepare apple-horseradish. Peel, seed and grate apples. Place in a small pot, add vinegar, sugar and cook over low heat for 10-12 min. Let cool. Stir in finely grated horseradish and season to taste.

● Clean and chop chives. Remove meat to a heated serving platter. Strain stock through a fine sieve and add a pinch of nutmeg and salt to taste. Slice meat across the grain and pour a little of the stock over it. Garnish with chives and boiled vegetables, if desired. Serve with apple horseradish and potatoes.

Serve with:
Potatoes

Viennese Coacher's Gulasch

(Wiener Fiakergulasch)

approx. 2 lbs beef (for roasting)
approx. 1½ lbs onions
2 T shortening or oil
2 T sweet paprika powder
1 T vinegar
approx. 3 cups (24 oz) beef stock
1 garlic clove, crushed
pinch of marjoram
½ tsp ground caraway
1 garlic clove, crushed
salt
pepper
1 T tomato paste
4 eggs
4 frankfurters
4 pickles (garnish)

● Rinse beef under cold water and pat dry with paper towel. Cut into large cubes. Peel onions and chop finely. Melt shortening in a large skillet and sauté onions until golden brown. Sprinkle with paprika powder; add vinegar and several tablespoons of beef stock.

● Add cubed meat and seasonings. Reduce heat, cover and simmer for about 1½ hours, stirring frequently and adding stock as needed.

● When meat is tender, add remaining stock, tomato paste and crushed garlic. Simmer for 10 more min. and season to taste.

● Spoon goulash into soup bowls and garnish with a fried egg, frankfurter and a gherkin cut in fan-form.

Serve with:
Fresh white rolls, steamed potatoes

F.Y.I.
The first official hackney driver („Fiaker") was licensed in Vienna in 1693. Today, the few remaining genuine coachers still wear their traditional costume: houndstooth trousers, velvet jacket and top hat. Just as unique is the goulash that bears the Fiaker's name.

Goulash, or gulyas, originated in Hungary. It is one of the few dishes that actually improves with time - it's even better as a „leftover" than when freshly prepared!

Veal Birds in Mushroom Sauce

(Kalbsvögerl in Schwammerlsoße)

4 - 6 slices of veal	3 oz bacon, diced
salt, white pepper	stewed vegetables, approx. 3 oz
2 oz bacon (or barding fat)	
4 oz ground meat	approx. 1 cup (8 oz) meat stock
4 T cream	
1 egg yolk, beaten	Sauce:
1 medium onion, chopped	½ cup (4 oz) sour cream
pinch of thyme	1 - 2 T flour
1 garlic clove, crushed	approx. 4 oz cooked mushrooms
1 small onion, chopped	

● Trim the edges of ½-inch thick veal slices, rinse and dry. Pound the meat with a cleaver, rub with salt and pepper. Make the filling as follows: Finely chop bacon and sauté until golden brown; combine with ground meat in a bowl. Add cream, ½ the chopped onions, egg yolk, steamed vegetables, thyme and crushed garlic. Spread a thin layer of filling on each slice of meat. Roll the meat; secure with skewers or thread.

● Dredge the birds in flour. Sauté remaining onions with diced bacon. Then sauté the birds in the onion/bacon mixture until golden brown. Add stock and reduce heat. Cover and simmer for 40-50 min, until tender.

● Remove the birds; remove skewers or thread.

● To make pan gravy: Add flour to sour cream and stir until smooth. Add to pan juices and bring to a boil. Add mushrooms. Correct seasoning. Return birds to gravy for several min. Serve immediately.

F.Y.I.

Well into the 19th century, song birds, particularly larks, were popularly prepared in this fashion in many of Upper Austria's larger cities. „Birdcatchers" delivered the birds to wealthier households. These delicious veal birds were prepared by those who could not afford the „real thing."

Crispy Roast Hock
(Knusprig gebratene Stelze)

1 large veal or pork hock, weighing approx. 2 ½ - 3 lbs	Root vegetable combination:
salt, pepper	1 onion
1 - 2 cloves of garlic	2 carrots
1 oz shortening	¼ celery root
approx. 1 cup hot water	salted water for basting

● Rinse hock briefly under cold, running water and pat dry with paper towel. Using a sharp knife, score thick skin all the way around the hock. Season and rub with pressed garlic.

● Preheat oven to 375° F.

● Melt shortening in an oven-resistant pan and brown hock. Douse with water and bake hock in oven for 1½ - 2 hours. Continue turning hock at regular intervals, basting occasionally.

● After about half of baking time has passed, add root vegetables.

● Shortly before end of baking time, baste with salted water and broil for several min to obtain crisp skin.

● Remove baking pan, place meat on a platter and keep warm in turned-off oven. Add some water to roasting pan juices. Strain and if necessary, bring briefly to a boil. Season to taste. Serve separately from meat.

● Serve hock whole or slice parallel to bone, replacing slices for serving. Arrange on a platter or wooden board.

Serve with:
Viennese Bread Dumpling or hearty rye bread, cabbage salad

Deep-Fried Veal Sweetbreads
(Gebackener Kalbsbries)

1 lb veal sweetbreads	2 - 3 T flour
salted water	4 - 5 T bread crumbs
salt, white pepper	2 oz shortening or oil for frying
1 - 2 eggs, beaten with salt and 1 - 2 T milk	
	4 lemon slices

● Thoroughly clean sweetbreads in cold water, then blanch. To do so, place sweetbreads in cold salted water. Bring to a boil. Simmer for about 5 min. Remove sweetbreads from pot and rinse under cold water. Carefully remove skins.

● Cut into ½-inch thick slices and season with salt and pepper. Dredge in flour, dip in egg/milk mixture and then bread crumbs.

● Heat oil or shortening in a large skillet. Place breaded lights in oil and reduce heat. Slowly fry slices until golden brown on both sides. Serve garnished with lemon slices.

Serve with:
Viennese Potato Salad or Lamb's Lettuce Salad

Crispy Leg of Lamb

(Knusprig gebratener Lammschlegel)

1 leg of lamb, with bone (approx. 3 lbs)
2 - 3 cloves of garlic
salt
freshly ground pepper
rosemary
2 - 3 T oil
2 tsp hot mustard
2 - 3 oz shortening
approx. 1 cup beef broth
$^1/_3$ - $^1/_2$ cup cream
2 T cold butter

● Remove skin and fat from leg of lamb. Rinse briefly under cold, running water and pat dry with paper towel.

● Peel and carefully quarter garlic cloves. With a pointed knife, make ½-inch holes in meat and insert quartered garlic cloves. Season meat with salt, freshly ground pepper and rosemary. Mix oil with mustard and rub onto meat on all sides.

● Preheat oven to 350° F.

● Melt shortening in a large roasting pan. Brown meat on all sides. Douse with beef broth and place in oven. Roast for 1½ - 2 hours, basting occasionally. Turn once. Remove from roasting pan and place on platter.

Return platter to turned-off oven to rest. Keep warm until served.

● Add water to loosen pan drippings. If necessary, strain through a sieve. Bring to a boil and add cream. Season to taste. Stir in cold butter. Cut meat along bone.

Serve sauce separately.

Serve with:
Green beans sautéed with onions, roasted potatoes.

Farmer's Platter
(Bauernschmaus)

4 - 6 slices smoked pork (to be fried)	1 lb sauerkraut
salt	juniper berries
ground caraway	4 frankfurters
shortening	4 slices roast pork (loin, shoulder) (prepared ahead of time)
1/8 lb bacon	bread dumplings
1 small onion	pickles

● Rinse smoked pork slices under cold, running water. Pat dry with paper towel. Season. Brown on both sides in melted butter/lard, reduce heat and continue warming.

● Dice bacon and brown in a large pot. Peel and finely chop onion. Add to bacon. Then add sauerkraut. Season, stir, cover and simmer until tender.

● Make two crossed 1-inch slices in ends of frankfurters. Place frankfurters on top of sauerkraut to heat. Prepare Bread Dumplings according to recipe on p. 52.

● Arrange on rustic wooden trencher in the following order: Pile sauerkraut in middle. Place one bread dumpling in the middle and arrange meat around dumpling. Decorate with fan-cut pickles.

Ground Veal Schnitzels
(Faschiertes Butterschnitzel)

2 stale rolls or 4 slices of white bread	1 lb ground veal (from shoulder)
2 eggs	salt, white pepper
approx. ½ cup lukewarm milk	pinch freshly ground nutmeg

approx. ½ cup bread scrumbs

5 - 6 T butter

5 - 6 T beef broth

● Cut rolls or white bread into small pieces. Place in a bowl and cover with milk. Let stand until soft.

● In a second bowl, combine ground veal with eggs, seasoning and pieces of roll out of which the milk has been squeezed. Mix well. Add bread crumbs to the mixture as needed to make a formable, still soft, consistency.

● Form 8 balls. Press into oval, ½-inch thick „schnitzels."

● Heat half of butter in large skillet. Place meat slices in butter and immediately reduce heat. Fry on both sides until golden brown (about 15 min).
Remove from pan and place on warmed platter. Cover and keep warm.

● Put beef broth in a pan, heat and stir in remaining butter. Reduce by cooking for several min.

● Place schnitzels on warmed plates, cover with sauce and serve immediately.

Paprika Chicken
(Paprikahuhn)

2 ½ - 3 lbs chicken (cleaned)

2 oz shortening

1 large onion, finely chopped

salt, ½ cup flour

1 T sweet paprika powder

1 cup sour cream

2 cups beef stock

● Thoroughly clean chicken inside and out. Pat dry with paper towel and cut into pieces.

● Melt shortening and brown chicken and onions. Season with paprika and

salt. Dust with flour and stir in sour cream.

● Cover with beef stock and simmer until done, stirring occasionally. Season to taste before serving.

Viennese Fried Chicken
(Wiener Backhendl)

2 small chickens, approx. 2 lbs each
2 eggs, lightly beaten
2 T cream
salt
white pepper
pinch of sweet paprika powder
4 oz flour
5 oz bread crumbs
9 oz shortening or ½ cup oil
2 lemon wedges or slices
parsley to garnish

● Clean and quarter fresh chicken, rinse under cold water and pat dry with paper towel. Remove skin; remove ribs and cartilage from breast pieces. Beat eggs, heavy cream, salt, pepper and paprika in a small, deep bowl. Put flour and bread crumbs on separate plates.

● Lightly salt chicken

pieces. First dredge in flour and shake off excess. Then dip in egg batter until completely coated. Finally, dredge in bread crumbs. Shake off excess crumbs.

● Heat oil or shortening slowly in a heavy, deep skillet. Place breaded chicken pieces in oil and fry for 10-15 min, until golden brown. Gently lift

and rotate the pan to ensure that oil reaches all parts of the chicken.

● Remove chicken pieces and drain on absorbent paper. If you need to keep chicken warm, cover with aluminum foil or place in warm oven. To serve, place on warmed platter. Garnish with lemon wedges and parsley.

Serve with:
Potato salad, optionally garnished with sliced cucumber, is an ideal side dish.

Oven-Browned Ham-Noodle Casserole - Old Vienna Style

(Überbackene Schinkenfleckerl)

Noodle dough:

⅞ cup flour, 2 eggs, salt
some flour for rolling out noodles
salt and 1 tsp oil for cooking water

To bake:

¾ lb boiled ham
1 medium onion
2 tsp butter
butter to grease casserole dish
3 eggs
½ cup sour cream
salt, white pepper, freshly ground nutmeg
2 T butter, bread crumbs if desired

● Noodles: Sift flour into a large bowl. Make a depression in the middle of the flour and add eggs and pinch of salt. Knead to a smooth dough. If necessary, add a bit of water so that all ingredients bind well. Continue kneading dough until it has a silky sheen. Cover and let stand for about 30 min. Then roll out on floured surface to the thickness of the back of a knife and let dry for about 10 min.

● In a large pot, bring water to a boil

● Cut dough into ½ - to

¾-inch noodle squares (first cut ½-inch strips in one direction, then ½-inch strips in the other).

● Add salt and oil to boiling water. Place noodle squares in water and cook for about 8 min until „al dente." Drain and rinse under cold, running water. Drain well.

● Finely dice ham.

● Heat butter in a skillet and sauté onions until translucent. Add diced ham and fry together briefly. Stir together eggs and sour cream. Season well.

● Grease a large oven-proof casserole dish. Sprinkle with bread crumbs. Put noodle squares in a large bowl. Combine with ham-onion mixture. Place in casserole dish and cover with egg-sour cream mixture. Dot with butter and bread crumbs if desired.

● Bake at 350° F for about 1 hour until golden brown. Serve in casserole dish or portion onto plates.

Serve with:
Mixed green salad.

Our tip:
Instead of making the noodles yourself, you can also use 300 g precooked flat egg noodles.

F.Y.I.
This dish belongs to the traditional „Old Vienna" cuisine. It can be found on many a menu in restaurants throughout the city. When preparing this dish, it's important to cut the noodles into the traditional squares to create the typical „Fleckerl."

Crackling Dumplings with Sauerkraut
(Grammelknödel mit Sauerkraut)

Dumpling dough:	
1½ lbs potatoes	
⁷/₈ cup flour, ¼ cup fine semolina	
2 T softened butter, 1 egg	
2 egg yolks	
1 pinch freshly grated nutmeg, salt	

Sauerkraut:
¾ lb sauerkraut
1 medium onion
¼ lb lean bacon

2 T butter	
1 bay leaf	
6 peppercorns	
½ cup beef broth	

Filling:
¼ lb cracklings
1 onion
2 - 3 T butter
2 T chopped parsley
1 clove of garlic
salt, pepper

● Boil potatoes in their skins. Peel and pass through potato press while still warm. Let cool somewhat, then add flour, semolina, butter, egg, yolks and seasoning. Use a mixer or food processor to blend to a smooth dough.

● Let stand for 10 - 15 min.

● To prepare sauerkraut, peel and finely chop onion.

Finely dice bacon. Melt butter in a large pot and fry onions and bacon. Then add sauerkraut, bay leaf and peppercorns.

● Add beef broth and simmer sauerkraut for 30 - 45 min until tender. Stir occasionally.

● To prepare filling: Finely chop cracklings. Fry with chopped onion in butter. Add chopped parsley, then pressed garlic and other seasonings. Season well. Remove from heat and let cool. Form 12 small balls.

● Shape potato dough into a long roll on floured surface. Cut into 12 slices and press each flat. Place a ball of filling onto each slice and shape dough around filling to form a dumpling.

● In a large pot, bring salted water to a boil. Gently add dumplings and reduce heat. Depending on the size of the dumplings, simmer for 14 - 18 min, until done.

● Remove dumplings with a slotted spoon. Arrange on plates and serve with sauerkraut.

F.Y.I.
Instead of cracklings for the filling, you can also use ¾ lb very finely minced roasted meats. The dumplings are then called „stuffed dumplings." Cooking time remains the same.

Palffy Bread Dumplings
(Serviettenknödel)

8 stale Kaiser rolls	2 T butter
1 cup lukewarm milk	1 linen napkin or kitchen towel
4 eggs	
pinch of freshly grated nutmeg	wooden spoon
	string
salt	some butter for basting
white pepper	8 - 12 cups salted water for boiling
3 - 4 T chopped parsley	

● Dice rolls and place in large bowl. Combine lukewarm milk with eggs and seasonings. Pour over rolls. Fry parsley in butter and add to bowl. Mix all ingredients well and let stand about 30 min.

● Bring salted water to a boil.

● Use wet hands to shape mixture into a long roll. Place on a linen napkin or kitchen towel, that has first been greased with butter. Roll mixture up in towel (loosely, so that it can expand during cooking). Tie both ends of napkin with string. Suspend from a long wooden spoon.

● Carefully suspend dumpling in towel/napkin in boiling water. Cover and let simmer for 50 - 60 min.

● Remove dumpling from water. Rinse quickly under cold water and remove towel/napkin. Let stand for several min. Cut into thick slices, arrange on warmed platter and serve immediately.

F.Y.I.
The idea of wrapping dumpling dough in a napkin or kitchen towel comes from Bohemia. It is suspected that the dumpling was first made at the palace of Count Palffy in Prague. It later became popular in Vienna, and the Palffy Dumpling was often served with various meat dishes.

Viennese Bread Dumplings
(Wiener Semmelknödel)

8 - 10 stale Kaiser rolls	salt
1 small onion	white pepper
2 - 3 T chopped parsley	pinch of freshly ground nutmeg
3 T butter	2 - 3 T flour if needed
1 cup lukewarm milk	12 cups salted water for cooking
3 - 4 eggs	

● Thinly slice stale rolls and briefly fry in butter with finely chopped onions and parsley. Place in a large bowl.

● Combine milk, eggs and seasonings. Pour over roll mixture. Knead and let stand for about 20 min. If needed, add flour and mix gently.

● With wet hands, shape dumplings and gently place in boiling salted water. Reduce heat and simmer dumplings gently for 12 - 15 min, depending on their size.

● Use a slotted spoon to remove from water. Serve immediately.

Viennese-Style Cabbage
(Kohl nach Wiener Art)

1 large head of cabbage (about 2 lbs)	white pepper
some salt	1 onion, chopped
4 raw potatoes	1 oz lard
1 clove of garlic, pressed	1/8 cup flour
caraway	1/2 cup hot beef stock

● Cut head of cabbage into large pieces. Remove bad leaves, core and coarser ribs.

● Boil in salted water with cubed potatoes, caraway and pepper until tender. Drain.

● Sauté garlic and onion in hot lard. Dust with flour and mix. Douse with broth. Add cabbage mixture and briefly bring to a boil. Season to taste.

F.Y.I.
This is a very mild cabbage dish and is actually known as „Kelch." It can be served with boiled beef, but is also eaten with fried sausages.

Viennese Potato Salad
(Wiener Erdäpfelsalat)

1 lb salad potatoes	1½ T vinegar
salt	white pepper
1 cup warm beef broth	pinch of sugar
1 small onion	freshly chopped chives
2 T corn oil	

● Boil potatoes in their skins. Drain, let cool somewhat. Peel and slice into a large bowl while still warm. Salt and pour in warm beef broth. Stir in chopped onion, oil, vinegar, salt, pepper and sugar. Mix well.

● Serve generously sprinkled with chopped chives.

F.Y.I.
You can also add greens or thinly sliced pickles to the potato salad. It is important to use solid salad potatoes for this dish.

Risi-Pisi
(Rice with Peas)

1 cup rice	2 T butter
2 cups water	½ cup precooked green peas
1 small onion	
2 whole cloves	1 heaping T grated Parmesan cheese
salt	

● Rinse rice under cold water and let drain. In a pot, bring rice, water and the onion with cloves inserted, salt and 1 T butter to a boil once. Reduce heat, cover and simmer about 25 min until tender.
● Remove onion. Leave rice uncovered so that steam can escape. Add remaining butter, then stir in peas and Parmesan cheese.

Green Beans with Bread Crumbs
(Fisolen mit Bröseln)

½ lb green beans	¼ lb butter
1 cup bread crumbs	salt, white pepper

● Wash and clean green beans. If necessary, pull off strings. Boil in salted water until tender. Drain and place in serving bowl.

● In a large skillet, melt butter, add and brown bread crumbs, season and distribute onto green beans. Serve immediately.

Mushroom Goulash
(Schwammerlgulasch)

1 lb fresh mushrooms	2 - 3 tsp flour, some paprika powder
5 T butter	
salt, white pepper	1 cup sour cream
1 tsp lemon juice	parsley

● Clean, rinse and finely slice mushrooms. Sauté quickly in butter. Season, dust with flour and paprika.

Add sour cream.
● Simmer briefly and serve topped with chopped parsley.

Cauliflower with Bread Crumbs
(Karfiol mit Butterbröseln)

1 large cauliflower (about 2 lbs)	pinch of freshly ground nutmeg
8 - 12 cups salted water for boiling	7 T butter, 4 - 6 T bread crumbs
2 cups milk	salt, white pepper

● Clean cauliflower, removing green leaves. Rinse well under cold, running water.
● In a large pot, bring water, salt, milk and nutmeg to a boil. Place cauliflower in the pot and simmer for 20 - 30 min until tender.
● Remove cauliflower with a slotted spoon and let drain. Arrange on a warmed platter.
● In a large skillet, melt butter and add bread crumbs. Brown, season and sprinkle onto cauliflower.
Serve immediately.

Lamb's Lettuce Salad
(Vogerlsalat)

½ lb fresh Lamb's Lettuce	4 - 6 T corn oil
1 chopped onion	freshly chopped herbs to taste
2 T lemon juice or vinegar	
salt, white pepper	½ clove pressed garlic

● Clean Lamb's Lettuce, removing any bad leaves. Rinse thoroughly 2 - 3 times under cold, running water. Drain well.

● In a large bowl, combine chopped onion with lemon juice or vinegar, and herbs.

● Then add oil and garlic.

Stir well, add greens and herbs. Mix quickly.

Variation:
Chicken cutlets with Lamb's Lettuce (photo), which goes well with many meat and fish dishes. You can also combine it with small chicken cutlets. To serve 4, you would need about 1 lb fresh chicken breast. Bread and fry 8 - 12 min in hot oil.

Pudding with Wine Sauce
(Saftiger Weinkoch)

4 egg yolks	½ T ground cinnamon
⅓ cup sugar	4 egg whites
juice and grated rind of 1 untreated lemon	butter for greasing pan
	Sauce:
½ cup (4 oz) ground almonds	1 cup dry red wine
½ cup bread crumbs	½ cinnamon stick
½ T bread crumbs	¼ cup sugar
	2 T cornstarch

● Beat egg yolks with sugar until foamy. Add lemon juice and grated rind, ground almonds, bread crumbs and cinnamon. Combine well. Beat egg whites until stiff and gently fold into mixture. Butter a large, oven-proof form and pour in batter. Smooth surface with a knife.

● Preheat oven to 325° F.

Bake for 30 - 40 min.

● To prepare sauce: Bring red wine, cinnamon stick and sugar to a boil. Stir cornstarch into some cold water, add to sauce and cook until thick. Remove cinnamon stick.

● Tip cake out onto a plate. Pour half of sauce over the cake. Serve remaining sauce separately.

Emperor's Pancake
(Kaiserschmarrn)

2 oz raisins
2 - 3 T rum
5 oz flour
pinch of salt
1 T powdered sugar, sifted
½ tsp vanilla extract
grated rind of ½ lemon
3 egg yolks, lightly beaten
3 egg whites
4 oz (½ cup) milk
1 tsp lemon juice
2 oz ground almonds (optional)
2 - 3 oz butter or margarine
2 T powdered sugar, sifted (for decoration)

● Stew raisins, drain and drizzle with rum. Sift flour into large bowl. Beat in salt, powdered sugar, vanilla, grated lemon rind, egg yolks and milk, until smooth. Let stand 20-30 min.

● Beat egg whites with powdered sugar and a few drops of lemon juice until very stiff. If desired, add ground almonds. Fold whites into batter.

● Melt butter in a large skillet. Pour in batter, sprinkle with raisins. Cover. Heat until underside is golden brown. Turn. Using two forks, gently pull pancake into bite-sized pieces and complete

cooking, stirring and
turning pieces often.
Serve hot, sprinkled
generously with powdered
sugar.

Our tip:
Serve „Kaiserschmarrn"
with cranberries, apple
sauce or stewed fruits. Eat
as a main dish or, in smaller
portions, as dessert.

F.Y.I.
According to legend, the
court chef dedicated this
dish to Empress Elizabeth,
wife of Austrian Emperor
Franz Josef I, calling it
the „Empress Pancake"
(Kaiserinschmarrn).
Since it was not to her
liking, but instead
satisfied the Emperor's
sweet tooth, it was simply
renamed.

Viennese Apple Strudel

(Alt-Wiener Apfelstrudel)

Strudel dough:

7 oz flour, sifted
1 egg, lightly beaten
1 T oil
pinch of salt
approx. 3 oz (⅓ cup) water

Filling:

3 oz raisins
2 T rum
2 oz butter, softened
3 ½ lbs cooking apples
4 oz sugar
pinch of cinnamon
3 - 4 oz (½ cup) bread crumbs
approx. 4 oz butter, softened
2 - 3 T powdered sugar, sifted (for decoration)

● Dough:
Sift flour into a bowl. Make a depression in the middle and drop in egg, oil and salt. Add water gradually while slowly beating the dough until it forms a medium-firm ball. Knead by hand for 10 min. more, until the dough has a silky sheen. Let stand about 30 min.

● Filling:
Drizzle rum over raisins and let stand. Peel and seed apples, slice thinly. Stir in cinnamon and sugar.

● Spread a clean tablecloth

or sheet on a large table. Sprinkle with flour and roll dough out as thin as possible. Stretch the dough gently from the center out using the backs of your hands, lightly clenched, palms down, moving around the table. Cut off thicker edges and use to patch if necessary.

● Preheat oven to 400° - 425° F. Grease baking sheet. Sprinkle bread crumbs on dough. Cover $2/3$ of the dough with apple filling and raisins. Fold sides of dough in over filling. Using the cloth, gently roll dough over itself, jelly-roll fashion, until filling is enclosed. Use cloth to slide strudel onto baking sheet. Baste with melted butter. Bake for 45 - 55 min, basting occasionally with butter. Dust with powdered sugar before serving.

Skillet Bread Pudding with Wine Chaudeau (Foamy Wine Sauce)

(Semmelschmarrn mit Weinchaudeau)

For bread pudding:

8 stale Kaiser rolls or white bread
4 eggs, 2 - 3 T sugar
2 cups lukewarm milk
6 T shortening
2 tsp cinnamon to sprinkle over bread pudding

For the Wine Chaudeau:

3 egg yolks
½ cup sugar
⅛ cup (1 oz) cornstarch
2 cups dry white wine
juice and rind of ½ untreated lemon

● Finely slice stale rolls and place in a large bowl. Combine milk and eggs and pour over rolls. Stir and let stand for about 30 min.

● Heat half of shortening in a large skillet. Pour in roll/milk mixture and let brown over medium heat. Turn over. Pull apart with a fork. Add remaining shortening and continue frying until golden brown.

● Sprinkle with sugar. Turn again and let sugar caramelize.

● Turn out onto a platter and sprinkle with cinnamon.

● For the Wine Chaudeau:

Beat egg yolks and sugar until creamy. Add cornstarch, wine, lemon juice and rind. In a double boiler or in a pan over low heat, stirring constantly, beat with a wire whisk until mixture thickens. Do not boil. Serve warm or cold with Skillet Bread Pudding.

Yeast Dumpling with Poppy Seeds
(Germknödel mit Mohn)

9 oz (1 cup and 1 T) flour	4 oz prune preserves, 1 tsp rum
¼ cup (2 oz) milk	pinch of cinnamon
1 oz fresh yeast or 1 T (½ pkg) dried yeast, plus 1 tsp sugar	2 oz ground poppy seeds
pinch of salt	2½ oz powdered sugar, sifted
1 egg yolk	2½ oz brown butter
1 oz butter, softened	

● Sift flour into large bowl. In separate bowl, blend lukewarm milk, yeast and sugar; add to flour. Add salt, egg yolk and soft butter. Beat with dough hooks until smooth. Cover and let rise in a warm place for about 45 min.

● Mix prune preserves with rum and cinnamon.

● On a floured surface roll dough to a thickness of approx. ½ in. Divide dough into 4 - 8 equal pieces. Put one teaspoon of prune filling in the middle of each piece, fold dough over filling and roll in floured hands to form dumplings. Let rise for 20 min.

● Meanwhile bring approx.

3 qts. of water with salt to a boil in a large pot. Place dumplings into water and simmer over low heat, turning after about 6-8 min. (total time: 12-16 min). Use a slotted spoon to remove. Drain gently, serve and place on plates.

● Sprinkle with ground poppy seeds and powdered sugar; drizzle with brown butter.

Our tipps:
To check whether dumplings are done, insert a toothpick. If no dough sticks to the toothpick, the dumplings are done. These yeast dumplings can also be prepared over steam. Place a clean, moist dish towel that has been basted with butter over a large pot of boiling water. The dumplings are placed on the towel and covered with a bowl. Cooking time: approx. 14 - 18 min.

Austrian Bread Pudding
(Scheiterhaufen)

8 stale rolls or white bread	½ cup sugar, 2 tsp rum
2 cups lukewarm milk	grated rind of 1 untreated lemon
softened butter for greasing casserole dish	
	½ cup raisins
4 T soft butter	¼ cup chopped hazelnuts
4 egg yolks	1 lb apples
4 egg whites	2 T butter, for dotting top

● Finely dice rolls and place in large bowl. Cover with milk and let stand for about 30 min.

● Preheat oven to 350° - 375° F.

● Grease a large casserole dish. In a bowl, combine butter, sugar, egg yolks, rum and grated lemon rind to a creamy batter. Stir in softened rolls, raisins and hazelnuts.

● Peel, quarter, core,
and finely slice apples.
Combine with roll mixture.
Beat egg whites until stiff
and fold into roll mixture.
Pour into casserole dish
and dot with butter. Bake
for 40 - 50 min until golden
brown.

Our tip:
In Vienna, the Kaiser rolls
are often replaced with
crescent rolls for the
popular „Kipferlkoch."
Because these are already
sweet, you can reduce
the amount of sugar used
to 40 g.

Sweet Cheese Strudel with Cream Sauce

(Millirahmstrudel mit Kanarimilch)

Strudel dough:

9 oz flour
pinch of salt
2 T melted butter or 2 T oil
1 egg
about ¼ cup lukewarm water
butter or oil to baste dough
softened butter to baste strudel

Filling:

½ cup raisins
6 - 7 stale Kaiser rolls or white bread
½ cup lukewarm milk
¼ lb (8 T) softened butter
½ cup sugar
5 egg yolks
pinch of salt
4 oz baker's cheese, well drained
½ cup sour cream
1 tsp vanilla extract
juice and rind of 1 small, untreated lemon
5 egg yolks, 2 T sugar
2 T butter to grease pan

Sauce for baking:

1 cup lukewarm milk
1 T sugar
1 tsp vanilla extract
2 egg yolks

Vanilla Sauce (when serving)

2 cups milk
2 egg yolks
marrow of ½ vanilla bean
scant ½ cup sugar

● For the strudel dough, follow instructions for Viennese Apple Strudel (p. 60). Cover and let stand for 30 min.

● In the meantime, prepare filling. First, wash and drain raisins. Cut rinds off rolls or white bread and dice finely. Place in a bowl and moisten with milk.

● Beat egg yolks, butter and sugar until creamy. Add salt, baker's cheese, sour cream, vanilla and grated lemon rind. In another bowl, beat egg whites, sugar and lemon juice until stiff, then fold into cream mixture.

Press excess milk from rolls and combine well with cream mixture, using a fork.

● Preheat oven to 350° F.

● Roll dough out onto a floured baking sheet or large kitchen towel. Spread filling evenly over dough, leaving a 1½-inch border of dough all around. Sprinkle with raisins.

● Using the cloth, roll dough up jelly-roll style. With the dough seam toward the bottom, place strudel in a large, greased pan (long bread pan). Baste with melted butter.

● Total baking time: 50 - 60 min, until golden-brown. For the baking sauce, beat together all ingredients and pour over strudel after it has baked about 20 min.

● Prepare vanilla sauce: Stir together milk and egg yolks, vanilla marrow and sugar. Whisk and heat slowly over medium heat. Do not boil.

● Remove strudel from oven and let stand for several min. Sprinkle generously with powdered sugar. Serve with warm vanilla sauce.

Viennese Fan Crepes with Strawberries and Ice Cream
(Fächerpalatschinken mit Erdbeeren und Eiscreme)

Prepare crepes according to recipe on page 70.

Fresh strawberries	Liqueur to taste (Grand Marnier, Cointreau, etc.)
Vanilla ice cream	Fresh mint leaves

● Place freshly made crepes like fans on dessert plates. Garnish with strawberries. Purée several strawberries with liqueur in a food processor and pour over crepes as a fruit sauce.
● Add one scoop of vanilla ice cream per plate. Garnish with fresh mint leaves and serve.

Crepes with Chocolate
(Palatschinken mit Schokolade)

Prepare crepes according to recipe on page 70.

5 oz grated chocolate	1 cup whipped cream
	sugar

● Sprinkle half of the grated chocolate on freshly made crepes. Roll crepes and arrange on dessert plates. Sprinkle with remaining chocolate and serve topped with sweetened whipped cream.

Crepes with Nut Filling
(Palatschinken mit Nussfülle)

Prepare crepes according to recipe on page 70.

½ cup ground hazelnuts	pinch of cinnamon
¼ cup sugar	6 - 8 T whipping cream

● Mix ground nuts with cinnamon and sugar. Add whipping cream until you have a creamy batter. Spread filling onto freshly made crepes. Roll and serve warm.

Sweet Cheese Crepes
(Topfenpalatschinken)

Basic Crepe Recipe:

1 cup (9 oz) flour
4 eggs
1½ cup milk
¼ tsp salt
oil for frying

Filling:

3 T soft butter
¼ cup sugar
3 eggs, separated
12 oz baker's cheese
1 tsp vanilla extract
pinch of salt
grated rind of ½ untreated lemon
1 T lemon juice
¼ cup raisins
powdered sugar to sprinkle over crepes

● For the filling:
Beat together butter, sugar and egg yolks. Stir in well-drained baker's cheese, vanilla, salt, grated lemon rind and lemon juice. In a separate bowl, beat egg whites until stiff and fold into cheese mixture. Finally, add raisins (rinse and pat dry before adding).

● Use an electric mixer to combine flour, eggs, milk and salt into a smooth batter. Let stand at least 30 min.

● In a medium-sized skillet, heat oil or shortening.

Using a ladle, pour in ¹/₈ of batter. Rotate skillet to spread batter thinly over entire floor. Over medium heat, fry crepe, turn when one side is golden brown. Make a total of 8 crepes, nicely browned on both sides.

● Spread cheese filling on each crepe. Roll and sprinkle generously with powdered sugar and serve.

F.Y.I.

„Palatschinken" have been a staple of Viennese cuisine since the 19th century. These thin pancakes originated in Romania, where they were called „placinta" or „flat cakes."
The Hungarians changed the name to „palacinta." When these delicious pancakes arrived in Vienna, they became the beloved „palatschinken."

Filled Sweet Rolls
(Dukatenbuchteln)

1 lb flour, salt	6 T soft butter
1 oz yeast	grated rind of ½ untreated lemon
scant cup of lukewarm milk	¼ lb butter for baking
1 egg, ½ cup sugar	apricot or prune preserves for the filling
1 tsp vanilla extract	

● Sift flour and salt into a large bowl. Form a depression in the middle. Crumble yeast into depression, add some milk and sugar. Stir and let stand in a warm location for 20 - 30 min.

● Add remaining milk, remaining sugar, egg, butter and grated lemon rind. Stir to form a smooth dough that releases easily from the edge of the bowl.

● Place dough on a floured surface. Roll until about 1 inch thick. Cut into small squares. Place ½ to 1 teaspoon of preserves in the center of each square and fold dough around filling.

● Butter a large baking pan or casserole dish. Place rolls in pan, seam side down, touching one another. Cover and let rise for 15 - 20 min. In the meantime, preheat oven to 300° - 325° F.

● Generously baste tops of rolls with butter. Bake for about 45 min. During baking, baste once with butter.

● Remove from oven when golden brown.

Our tip:
Vanilla sauce is wonderful with these filled sweet rolls. Use the recipe on p. 66.

Nut „Noodles"
(Saftige Nussnudeln)

1 lb potatoes	some grated nutmeg
4 T butter	butter or lard
¾ cup flour	4 ½ oz ground nuts (walnuts or hazelnuts)
¼ cup fine semolina	
2 egg yolks	2 - 3 T sugar
pinch of salt	3 T powdered sugar

● Boil unpeeled potatoes until tender. Peel while still warm and press. Combine potatoes with butter, flour, semolina, egg yolk and salt to form a smooth dough. Let stand for 20 - 30 min.

● Bring large pot of salted water to a boil.

● On a floured surface, roll dough into a long 1-inch thick oblong. Cut off walnut-sized pieces and roll each into a cigar-shaped cylinder, pointed at both ends.

● Drop „noodles" into gently boiling water and simmer for 8 - 10 min, depending on size, until done. Remove to a colander and drain well.

● In a high skillet, melt butter or lard. Stir in nuts and sugar. Add noodles and rotate pan until noodles are coated with nut mixture.

● Place on plates, sprinkle with powdered sugar and serve.

Viennese Chocolate Pudding
(Mohr im Hemd)

8 T soft butter
¾ cup sugar
4 egg yolks
4 egg whites
1 T lemon juice
3 oz melted bitter chocolate (baking chocolate)
1½ rolls, the crust grated off, softened in milk, drained, and puréed
¼ cup ground almonds
⅓ cup bread crumbs
softened butter and bread crumbs to grease fluted form
1 cup whipping cream
2 T sugar

● Combine butter with two-thirds of sugar and egg yolks until very creamy. Stir in melted chocolate, milk-moistened bread, ground almonds and dry bread crumbs.

● Beat egg whites until semi-stiff. Sprinkle in remaining sugar and several drops of lemon juice. Continue beating until very stiff. Carefully fold into chocolate mixture.

● Butter and coat inside of a heat-resistant fluted form with bread crumbs. Pour in

batter. Cover form. Place in boiling water for 1 hour. Let cool slightly and then turn out onto a platter.

● Serve with sweetened whipped cream.

Our tip:
If you don't have the special pudding mold, you can also use a fluted cake pan of metal or porcelain. Batter is poured into the greased and bread-crumbed form. Fill a deep frying pan with hot water (about 1½ qts), place pudding form in the water and cover with a large plate. Simmer for about 1½ hours, until done.

Bohemian Plum Cakes

with prune jam
(Böhmische Dalken)

Batter:

1 cup flour
1 oz yeast
2 T sugar
about 1 cup lukewarm milk
3 T butter
2 eggs
pinch of salt
grated rind of ½ untreated lemon
4 T shortening for baking
prune jam for filling
½ cup cinnamon sugar (to sprinkle over cakes)
rum

● Sift flour into a bowl. Make a depression in the center.

● Crumble yeast into the depression. Add lukewarm milk and sugar. Stir. Cover and let mixture stand in a warm place for about 20 min.

● Melt butter in remaining milk. Combine with eggs, salt and grated lemon rind. Gradually stir into flour mixture until a soft, thick batter results. Cover and let stand for another 15 - 20 min.

● Place some shortening in the bottoms of each of the depressions in a „Dalken" pan - similar to a poached egg pan, and heat. Place about 1 T of batter in each

hole, let brown, turn, and brown other side.

● Place one cake on a plate, spread with prune filling, which has been flavored with rum, and cover with a second cake. Sprinkle with powdered sugar and serve lukewarm.

F.Y.I.

The „Dalken" - also called „Flat Doughnuts" in Lower Austria - came to Vienna when Bohemia was still part of the Austrian Empire. If you do not have a special „Dalken" pan, reduce amount of milk in the batter to about ½ cup so that it isn't as soft. Roll dough out on a floured surface to about ¼ inch thickness. Use a glass to cut 3-inch rounds out of the dough. Let these rise, then fry in a large skillet until golden brown on both sides.

Prune-Filled Doughnuts

(Wiener Schlosserbuam)

¾ lb prunes	3 T oil
water, mixed with rum, for soaking	½ cup milk
	dry white wine or beer
¼ cup whole, shelled almonds	pinch of salt
pinch of cinnamon, mixed with sugar	2 T sugar
	2 egg whites
Batter:	6 cups vegetable shortening for frying
⅔ cup flour	¼ cup grated chocolate
2 egg yolks	¼ cup powdered sugar

● Soak the prunes over night, but at least for four hours, in cold water mixed with rum. Drain well. Score

prunes, remove pit and replace with one whole almond each. Sprinkle prunes with cinnamon-sugar mixture.

● For the dough, sift flour into a bowl. Add egg yolks, oil, liquid and salt and mix to a smooth batter. Let rest at least one hour. Beat egg whites until stiff and fold into batter.

● Heat shortening.

● Dip prunes into the batter to coat entirely. Using a slotted spoon, place prunes in hot shortening and fry until golden brown. Remove carefully and let drain on paper towel.

● Turn the dumplings in grated chocolate and powdered sugar until coated. Serve warm with strawberry sauce.

Vienna Maidens
(Wiener Wäschermadln)

12 ripe apricots	powdered sugar
3 ½ oz marzipan	6 cups shortening for frying
1 - 2 T apricot schnapps	
batter as for Prune-Filled Doughnuts	some sugar mixed with vanilla sugar

● Wash apricots, peel, score and carefully remove the pit. Replace with a small ball of marzipan. Sprinkle with apricot schnapps and powdered sugar. Let stand.

● Meanwhile, prepare batter as for Prune-Filled Doughnuts. Let rest.

● Dip apricots into batter,

fry in shortening until golden brown, let drain. Sprinkle with sugar mixture. Serve warm.

F.Y.I.
The „Vienna Maidens" are an old Carnival pastry that is popular with a „Mélange" (see Coffee Primer).

79

Delicate Mocha Crème
(Feine Mokkacreme)

2 egg yolks	1 packet clear gelatin powder
4 - 5 level T instant coffee	
2 cups milk	2 egg whites
1/3 cup sugar	1/2 cup whipping cream
1 tsp vanilla extract	chocolate coffee beans for garnish

● Beat together egg yolks, instant coffee and some milk. In a pan, slowly bring remaining milk, sugar, salt and vanilla extract to a boil. Remove from heat and quickly stir in egg yolk - coffee mixture, as well as the dissolved gelatin (prepare according to directions). Place in refrigerator.
● As soon as the mixture thickens, fold in stiffly beaten egg whites and whipped cream.
● Pour into a serving bowl. Cool until firm. Garnish with coffee beans.

Cheese Dumplings with Plums
(Topfenknödel mit Zwetschkenröster)

18 oz curd, baker's cheese or cottage cheese	4 oz (1/2 cup) bread crumbs roasted in
4 eggs	2 1/2 oz butter
4 1/2 oz (1/2 cup) bread crumbs	1 lb fresh or canned plums
4 oz (2/3 cup) sugar	2 T sugar
pinch of salt	pinch of cinnamon
1/2 tsp vanilla extract	1 T rum
	1 tsp lemon juice

● Drain cottage cheese and press through a sieve. Mix with eggs, bread crumbs, sugar, salt and vanilla extract until smooth. Let stand for about 45 min.
● With wet hands, form 2-inch dumplings. Drop

into boiling salted water, reduce heat and simmer gently for about 10 min. Brown bread crumbs in butter in a skillet. Transfer dumplings to skillet with slotted spoon and rotate gently to coat dumplings.

● Wash plums and cut in half, removing pits. In a small skillet, cook plums with sugar, cinnamon, rum and lemon juice. Serve separately.

Mock Saddle of Venison Cake with Pinenuts
(Rehrücken mit Pignoli)

8 T (¼ lb) soft butter	¼ cup cornstarch
1 cup powdered sugar	½ cup ground almonds
4 oz melted chocolate (melted in double boiler)	1 tsp baking power
	chocolate glaze
6 egg yolks	2 oz pinenuts (pignoli)
6 egg whites	butter and bread crumbs for form
⅓ cup sugar	
¼ cup flour	whipped cream

● Beat together butter and powdered sugar until creamy. Gradually drizzle in melted chocolate. Add egg

yolks and continue stirring.
● In a separate bowl, beat egg whites until stiff. Sprinkle in sugar teaspoon by teaspoon and continue beating until mixture forms stiff peaks. Fold into chocolate mixture. Sprinkle with ground almonds.
● Combine flour, cornstarch and baking powder. Sift over other ingredients and fold together.
● Butter long loaf pan and sprinkle with bread crumbs.
● Preheat oven to 325° F.
● Pour batter into loaf pan. Smooth and bake for 50 - 60 min. Let cool slightly in pan, then tip out onto grid.
● When cake has cooled, glaze with chocolate and decorate with pinenuts (to simulate larding of a saddle of venison). Serve with whipped cream.

Chocolate Pretzels
(Schokoladenbrezeln)

½ lb butter	½ lb flour
1 cup powdered sugar	½ cup cocoa
1 egg yolk, 4 T rum	16 oz chocolate glaze
pinch of salt	baking paper

● Stir together butter and powdered sugar. Add egg yolk. Sift flour and combine with cocoa powder. Stir into butter/sugar mixture.
● Cover dough and cool in refrigerator for at least 2 hours.
● Cut dough into 3 portions. Roll each out into an approx. 1-foot-long rope. Cut into 20 equally sized pieces. Roll these pieces out into thin ropes. Preheat oven to 325° F.
● Shape pretzels from thin ropes. Use egg white to glue ends together.
● Place finished pretzels on an ungreased cookie sheet or one lined with baking parchment. Do not place pretzels too close to one another. Bake for 8 - 11 min.
● Melt glaze in a double boiler and dip cooled pretzels in, one by one.
● Place on baking parchment and let glaze cool.
● Recipe makes about 60 pretzels.

Viennese Vanilla Crescents
(Wiener Vanillekipferl)

½ lb flour, ½ cup sugar

1 tsp vanilla extract

some vanilla marrow

3 egg yolks

½ cup ground almonds

¾ lb butter

4 - 5 T vanilla sugar for dusting crescents

● Quickly combine all ingredients to form a smooth dough. Place in refrigerator to cool for at least one hour.
● Roll dough into a thin rope. Cut small, equally sized pieces and from each, shape a crescent.

Place these on a greased cookie sheet or one lined with baking parchment.
● Bake in a 325° F oven for 12 - 14 min until golden brown. While still hot, dust with vanilla sugar.
● Recipe makes about 60 crescents.

Sacher Torte
(Sachertorte)

---

5 oz butter	
4 oz powdered sugar, sifted	
8 egg yolks	
5 oz dark chocolate	
5 oz (⅔ cup) flour	
8 egg whites	
2 oz sugar	
2 T apricot jam	
8 oz (1 cup) cream	
4 oz dark chocolate glaze	

● Cream softened butter and powdered sugar. Beat in egg yolks one after another until the mixture is thick and creamy. Melt bittersweet chocolate in a double boiler or microwave oven. Stir melted chocolate until lukewarm, then stir into cream by the teaspoonful. Sift in flour.

● Beat egg whites with sugar until stiff. Gently fold into chocolate mixture with a wire whisk.

● Line bottom of 9-inch spring form pan with baking paper circle. Spread batter evenly and bake in a 340° - 375° F oven for 50 - 65 min. Remove and let cool for several min. Run a knife around the cake and remove sides of pan. Let cake cool completely on wire rack. Remove paper and, if necessary,

even out cake bottom
with a knife.

● Stir and warm apricot
preserves. Smooth over
entire cake, including
sides.

● Melt commercial
chocolate glaze to
frost cake. Decorate
as desired. Serve with
whipped cream.

F.Y.I.
This recipe, though typical,
is not the one for the
„Original Sacher Torte,"
which is a heavily
guarded secret of
the Sacher Company.
In the peak season, over
2000 tasty tortes are
produced each day by
Sacher, Vienna, ready
for export to all corners
of the world.

Viennese Saverin Cake

(Wiener Savarin)

½ lb flour	7 oz apricot preserves and 1 T lemon juice to glaze
½ packet yeast	
scant 2 cups of lukewarm milk	For syrup:
6 T soft butter	1 cup water
¼ cup sugar	1 cup sugar
1 egg	juice of one orange
1 - 2 egg yolks	juice of one lemon
pinch of salt	1 whole clove
grated rind of ½ untreated lemon	¼ cinnamon stick
	⅛ cup rum

● Make a yeast dough as described below for „Carnival Doughnuts" (p. 94), adding grated lemon rind. Let rise.

● Grease and flour a 12-inch ring form.

● Roll dough out into a thick rope. Place in the ring form and let rise for another 20 min.

● Preheat oven to 325° F. Bake cake for 30 - 40 min. Let cool slightly and then tip cake out onto a platter.

● For syrup:
Combine water with all other ingredients (except rum) and bring to a boil until a clear syrup forms. Drain through a sieve and add rum.

● Pour syrup over cake. Then bring apricot preserves, lemon juice and some water to a boil. Whisk until smooth and puree or press through a sieve. Smooth over cake. Serve warm.

Viennese Cheese Stollen
(Wiener Topfenstollen)

9 oz baker's cheese	12 oz flour
10 T soft butter	4 oz cornstarch
½ cup sugar	4 level tsp baking powder
1 tsp vanilla extract	
½ level tsp salt	4 oz slivered almonds
grated rind of 1 untreated lemon	7 oz dried fruits
	2 T rum
½ level tsp cinnamon	melted butter for basting
1 egg	powdered sugar

● Combine cheese, soft butter, sugar, vanilla extract, salt, lemon rind, cinnamon, egg, flour, cornstarch and baking powder in a mixing bowl. Using the kneading attachment, knead until you have a smooth dough. Then add slivered almonds and dried fruit, which has been finely chopped and soaked in rum. Knead thoroughly.

● Roll dough out onto a floured surface. Form a stollen. Place on a greased baking sheet or one lined with baking parchment. Preheat oven to 325° F. Bake stollen for 50 - 60 min.

● While still hot, baste with melted butter and generously sprinkle with powdered sugar.

Bratislava Nut or Poppyseed Crescents
(Pressburger Nuss- oder Mohnbeugel)

Dough:	
¾ lb butter	
1 lb flour	
3 T sugar	
4 egg yolks	
1½ oz yeast	
6 - 7 T lukewarm milk	
pinch of salt	
1 - 2 egg yolks for basting	

Nut filling:	
½ cup (5 oz) ground hazelnuts	
⅓ cup sugar	
1 tsp vanilla extract	
6 T cream	

1 T bread crumbs	
1 T apricot preserves	
dash of rum	

Poppyseed filling:	
1 cup milk	
⅓ cup sugar	
1 T honey	
9 oz ground poppyseeds	
grated rind of 1 untreated lemon	
pinch of cinnamon (⅛ tsp.)	
1 T rum	
¼ cup raisins (optional)	
3 T bread crumbs	

● Sift flour into a bowl. Cut butter into small pieces and distribute over flour. Dissolve yeast into a mixture of lukewarm milk, sugar, egg yolk and salt. Stir until a smooth dough results. Cover and et rise for 30 min in a warm spot.

● In the meantime, prepare nut or poppyseed filling.

● For the nut filling: Combine all ingredients in the listed order. Use rum and apricot preserves to taste.

● For the poppyseed filling: Bring milk, sugar and honey to a boil. Add poppyseeds and let thicken. Stir in remaining ingredients.

● On a floured surface, roll dough out very thinly and cut into equally sized squares.

● Preheat oven to 300° F.

● Place nut or poppyseed filling on each square. Form these into crescents and coat with egg yolk.

● On a greased and floured cookie sheet, bake crescents until golden brown, about 20 - 25 min. Serve fresh.

Emperor's Kugelhupf
(Kaiserguglhupf)

14 oz (1 ¾ cups) flour	pinch of salt
4 oz (½ cup) ground almonds	4 oz (½ cup) cream
	3 oz raisins
1½ oz fresh yeast or 2 T (1 pkg) dried yeast, plus 1 T sugar	4 T rum
	grated rind of 1 untreated lemon
4 oz (½ cup) lukewarm milk	butter and bread crumbs or ground almonds for the baking pan
5 oz (⅔ cup) sugar	
5 oz butter	
5 eggs	1 T powdered sugar, sifted (for decoration)

● Blend sifted flour with ground almonds in a large bowl. Make a depression in the middle. Crumble in compressed yeast, lukewarm milk and several teaspoons of sugar. Stir and let rise in a warm place for about 15 min.

● Preheat oven to 350° - 400° F. Melt butter and beat with remaining sugar, eggs, salt and cream until very light and creamy.

● Stir in raisins, rum and grated lemon rind. Add this mixture to the yeast dough and beat well until smooth and elastic. Batter should pull away from the sides of the bowl.

● Grease a fluted tube pan and dust with bread crumbs. Pour in dough and bake for 60-70 min.

● Let cake cool in the pan. Turn it over onto a wire rack and dust top with powdered sugar.

Coffee Crème Torte with Cocoa
(Kaffeecremetorte mit Schoko)

Batter:

½ lb soft butter

1 cup sugar

1 tsp vanilla extract

pinch of salt

4 eggs, separated

7 oz flour

¼ cup cornstarch

1 tsp baking powder

Crème:

½ cup cream

pinch of salt

9 oz baker's chocolate (bitter-sweet)

½ lb butter

1 cup powdered sugar

grated chocolate and cocoa for sprinkling over cake.

● Beat together until very creamy butter, sugar, vanilla extract and salt. Add egg yolks. In a separate bowl, beat egg whites until stiff. Fold into butter mixture. Combine dry ingredients (flour, cornstarch, baking powder) and sift over butter mixture. Fold together lightly.

● Preheat oven to 300° F.

● Divide dough into 5 portions. Pour each into a greased 13-inch spring form and bake until golden brown, 15 - 20 min. Let cool.

● For the crème: Heat together cream and salt. Stir in baker's chocolate until melted. Place pot in ice water and let crème cool, stirring constantly.

● Beat together butter and powdered sugar and fold into cooled chocolate crème mixture.

● Spread crème filling onto four cake rounds, leaving some for frosting. Place cake rounds on top of one another, finishing with fifth round. Spread decoratively with remaining crème (top and sides).

● Chill. Sprinkle sides with grated chocolate and top with cocoa powder.

Carnival Doughnuts
(Feine Faschingskrapfen)

1 lb flour	¼ lb (8 T) soft butter
1½ oz yeast	16 oz shortening or lard for deep frying
⅓ - ½ cup sugar	
1 tsp vanilla extract	4 T apricot preserves for filling
salt	
about 1 cup lukewarm milk	powdered sugar for sprinkling
2 - 3 egg yolks	

● Sift flour into a large mixing bowl. Create a depression in the middle. Crumble yeast into the depression. Pour in some of lukewarm milk and sugar. Stir together, cover and let rest in a warm spot for 20 - 30 min.

● Stir in remaining milk, remaining sugar, vanilla extract, salt, egg yolk and soft butter to form a smooth dough that releases from the sides of the bowl. Use a food processor or mixer.

● Place dough on a floured surface and roll out about 1 inch thick. Use a glass to cut 4-inch rounds. Cover

with a dry towel and let rise for 15 -20 min.

● Heat shortening. Carefully drop in dough circles and brown for about 3 min on both sides, turning once or several times.

● Use a slotted spoon to remove doughnuts. Place on paper towels to drain.

● If desired, fill doughnuts with apricot preserves after they have cooled, using a special filling tool.

● Sprinkle generously with powdered sugar and serve.

Coffee Primer

When you order a cup of coffee in Munich or Paris, you'll get one quickly and without much ado. In Austria, however, coffee is more than a mere beverage: it is a tradition. Coffee is best enjoyed in one of Austria's countless coffeehouses. Enjoyment requires peace and quiet, and coffeehouses offer so much of it that it's even possible to read a newspaper without being constantly interrupted by a waiter requesting further orders. The waiter will only refill the mandatory glass of water without being asked.

In Austria, particularly Vienna, coffee is served in myriad ways. I would like to tell you about some of these specialties:

A „Pharisäer" (German for Pharisee), with its whipped cream cap, might look innocent, but be prepared - it's made with a large shot of rum. The „Konsul" (or consul) doesn't have anything to do with diplomacy; it consists of black coffee with a dash of cream. An „Einspänner" (one-horse carriage) is a double mocha, served in a tall glass with lots of whipped cream and topped with powdered sugar. After a good meal, a cup of **Turkish coffee** is preferred. Other Viennese coffee specialties are the **Maria Theresa Coffee**, which contains orange liqueur, and the „**Kaiser-Melange**" (Imperial Melange) with an egg yolk. The Austrian „**Kapuziner**" (capuccino) is made with strong espresso coffee, topped with whipped cream and dusted with cocoa powder.

The „**kleiner Braune**" (small espresso) and „**grosser Braune**" (large espresso) are two versions of coffee and cream. If some happens to be left over, let it cool, mix in some maraschino liqueur, pour over ice in a fancy glass and you have a „**Mazagran** ".

If you would like to offer your guests „**Kaffee mit Schleppe**", you must provide an appealing dessert or pastry with the coffee.

About the Recipes:
Most recipes serve four.
The desserts and pastries,
since they may also be
served as main dishes,
can serve more. Oven
temperatures are given
for ovens with top and
bottom heat. If you use a
convection oven, reduce
heat by about 50° F. Baking
times remain the same.

Guide to Abbreviations:
I have used the following
abbreviations or terms in
this book:

lb	pound
min	minute(s)
oz	ounce(s)
pt	pint
qt	quart
T	tablespoon(s)
tsp	teaspoon(s)

Photo Credits:
Front cover: Fotostudio
Teubner, Füssen
Austrian Tourism Promotion,
Vienna, pages: 2, 4, 11, 25,
63
Fotostudio Teubner,
Füssen: pages 12, 46, 82,
89, 91
Langnese-Iglo, Hamburg: 19
Orac Publishers, Gusto
Archive: pages 16, 27, 29,
49, 56, 66, 76, 78, 81
Wine from South Tyrol,
Tübke & Partners, Munich:
page 21

Sigloch Edition, Künzelsau:
pages 32, 34, 58, 70, 84
Komplettbüro, Munich:
pages 37, 44, 65, 68
Robert Bosch Household
Appliances, Munich: pages
38, 40, 54
Lower Austrian Milk Products
Aachen: 60, 93
Vitri GmhH, Mühltal: 74
Knorr-Maizena, Heilbronn: 87

The author and publishing
company would like to
express their thanks to the
above organizations for
providing an excellent
assortment of photographic
material.

Design and Production:
Verlagsbüro Fritz
Petermüller, Siegsdorf
Editorial Office: Ursula
Calis, Munich.
Translation: Mary Heaney
Margreiter

© **KOMPASS-Karten GmbH**
  Rum/Innsbruck 2008
Fax 0043 (0) 512/265561-8
E-mail: kompass@kompass.at
http://www.kompass.at
Publication No. 1716
ISBN 3-85491-805-9